Sex-Based Harassment

Workplace Policies for the Legal Profession

Second Edition

Commission on Women in the Profession
American Bar Association

ABA
Defending Liberty
Pursuing Justice

Cover design by ABA Publishing

11 10 09 08 07 5 4 3 2 1

Library of Congress Cataloging-in-Publication Data

Sex-based harassment.

p. cm.

Includes bibliographical references.

ISBN 978-1-59031-871-3

1. Sexual harassment—Law and legislation—United States. I. American Bar Association. Commission on Women in the Profession.

KF3467.S463 2007

344.7301'133—dc22 2007026162

Discounts are available for books ordered in bulk. Special consideration is given to state bars, CLE programs, and other bar-related organizations. Inquire at Book Publishing, ABA Publishing, American Bar Association, 321 North Clark Street, Chicago, Illinois 60610.

www.ababooks.org

Contents

Acknowledgments

This book represents a mutually rewarding partnership between the ABA Commission on Women in the Profession and the ABA Section of Labor and Employment Law. The Commission gratefully acknowledges the members of the revision committee—Patricia Costello Slovak (chair), Jana Howard Carey, Angie Davis, Vickie A. Gillio, Nancy E. Hoffman, Allegra J. Lawrence-Hardy, and Helen Norton—who generously donated their time and talent in creating this second edition of *Sex-Based Harassment*. Appreciation also goes to Nathan Chapman, Allison Cohen, Marshawn Evans, Kylie Holladay, Elena Parent, and Douglas Warren for their additional research. Special thanks to Keri Ambrose for her help in preparing the manuscript.

American Bar Association
Commission on Women in the Profession
321 N. Clark Street
Chicago, IL 60610
Phone: 312/988-5715
Fax: 312/988-5790
Web Site: www.abanet.org/women

Any proceeds from this publication will go toward the projects of the ABA Commission on Women in the Profession.

PART I

INTRODUCTION

Over the last three decades, sex-based harassment has become a matter of national concern. A wide array of research on employment, educational, and professional settings reveals that a significant number of women and men have experienced some form of sex-based harassment, and that the costs to both individuals and organizations are quite substantial.

Such harassment can have significant emotional, physical, and social consequences for lawyers, as well as serious consequences for legal employers in terms of lost productivity, increased turnover, impaired reputation, and greater risk of liability and litigation expenses.[1] Society in general, and the legal system in particular, also pay a price when harassing conduct compromises equal opportunity and undermines performance.

Growing awareness of these consequences underscores the need for effective policies and programs concerning sex-based harassment. Considerable progress has been made since the ABA Commission on Women in the Profession was founded in 1987, when only about a third of surveyed law firms had sexual harassment policies.[2] More recent studies indicate that the vast majority of legal employers, including public sector and educational employers, now have such policies.[3]

1. See sources cited below at notes 19-23.

2. *Looking Backward, Moving Forward*, PERSPECTIVES, Fall 1997; Thom Weidlich & Charise K. Lawrence, *Sex and the Firms: A Progress Report*, NAT'L L. J., Dec. 20, 1993, at 1.

3. Martha Neil, *Hidden Harassment: Law Firms and Disciplinary Authorities Look for Ways to Fight Sexual Misconduct*, 92 A.B.A. J. 43, 46 (2006) (growing number of law firms are implementing and fine-tuning new broad-based anti-discrimination programs that include education intended to prevent sexual harassment). Susan Saab Fortney, *Law Firm General Counsel as Sherpa: Challenges Facing the In Firm Lawyer's Lawyer*, 53 U. KAN. L.

Yet not all these policies are adequately designed or effectively implemented in practice. Almost three-quarters of women lawyers believe that harassment is a problem in their workplaces.[4] Reported cases make clear that plainly abusive conduct persists.[5]

The legal profession cannot expect to maintain public respect and credibility if it cannot ensure compliance with legal standards and equal opportunity in its own workplaces. Lawyers who engage in harassment impose costs upon their clients as well. Moral fitness is a condition precedent to becoming a lawyer and a requirement for the able advocate and attorney. A client who cannot rely upon his or her attorney's character cannot fully trust that attorney's expertise or judgment, either.

All lawyers thus have a stake in promoting more effective responses to sex-based harassment. This manual assists such initiatives.

A. The Definition and Prevalence of Sex-Based Harassment

The term "sexual harassment" came into use during the mid-1970s to describe two forms of gender discrimination: (1) quid pro quo

REV. 835, 851 (2005) (2004 Altman Weil, Inc. Survey on Law Firm General Counsel shows 52.94% of the respondents indicated they advised their firms on employment law matters, including discrimination, harassment, and terminations). Gail Schmoller Philbin, *The Unspoken Accusation: Decades into the Women's Movement, Victims of Sexual Harassment Are Still Suffering in Silence*, ORLANDO SENTINEL, Mar. 24, 2004, at G1; Minnesota Women Lawyer's Association, Self-Audit for Gender Equity (June 1999) (97% of firms have written policy); Dana Casale, *Area Firms Share Sexual Harassment and Anti-Discrimination Policies*, LAWYERS J., June 30, 2000, at 4.

4. Martha Neil, *Hidden Harassment: Law Firms and Disciplinary Authorities Look for Ways to Fight Sexual Misconduct*, 92 A.B.A. J. 43, 44 (2006); Eyana J. Smith, *Employment Discrimination in the Firm: Does the Legal System Provide Remedies for Women and Minority Members of the Bar?*, 6 U. PA. J. LAB. & EMP. L. 789, 800 (2004) (sexual discrimination also has had the devastating result among lawyers of forcing women to leave the law completely); Joanna Grossman, *Sexual Harassment in Law Firms: Why It Still Exists, and Why Firms Haven't Taken Steps to Prevent It and to Decrease Their Own Liability*, FINDLAW'S WRIT—LEGAL COMMENTARY, NOV. 11, 2000. Note, of course, that women—like men—may not only be victims of harassment, but may engage in it themselves.

5. *See* sources cited *infra* notes 8 and 23.

harassment that takes the form of unwelcome requests for sexual favors in exchange for job opportunities like hiring or promotion; and (2) hostile environment harassment, which includes conduct that sexualizes, demeans, or intimidates individuals on the basis of gender.[6] Sex-based harassment need not be sexual in nature to constitute illegal discrimination; conduct that reflects adverse gender-based stereotypes or animosity may also constitute illegal discrimination.[7] Sexual harassment thus encompasses a range of behaviors on the part of supervisors, co-workers, peers, clients, judges, professors, students, and vendors.[8]

Surveys continue to find that a significant percentage of female lawyers and court personnel report experiencing or observing sexual

---

6. Heather L. Kleinschmidt, *Reconsidering Severe or Pervasive: Aligning the Standard in Sexual Harassment and Racial Harassment Causes of Action,* 80 IND. L.J. 1119, 1134–35 (2005) ("After Congress passed the Civil Rights Act of 1964, federal courts hesitantly accepted sexual harassment as an actionable claim under Title VII. Prior to 1977, only five sexual harassment cases had been litigated under Title VII. Of these cases, only one held that sexual harassment was actionable under Title VII. It was not until the late 1970s that the tide began to turn for sexual harassment plaintiffs. Sexual harassment as a cause of action did not gain judicial recognition until 1976.").

7. As the Supreme Court has noted, sex harassment may be motivated by "gender-based animus" as well as "a desire to fulfill sexual urges." Burlington Indus., Inc. v. Ellerth, 524 U.S. 742, 765 (1998). *See also* Martha S. West, *Preventing Sexual Harassment: The Federal Courts' Wake-Up Call for Women,* 68 BROOK. L. REV. 457, 465 (2002) (judges and some commentators take view that the term "sexual harassment" covers all forms of harassment of women, both sexual and non-sexual). United States E.E.O.C. v. Continental Airlines, Inc., 2006 WL 14510, 17 N.D. Ill., 2006) (citing Smith v. Sheahan, 189 F.3d 529, 533 (7th Cir. 1999) (holding sex-based animus is sufficient for a Title VII claim)). Peterson v. Hewlett-Packard Co., 358 F.3d 599, 603 (9th Cir. 2004) (gender stereotyping violates Title VII). Nev. Dep't of Human Res. v. Hibbs, 538 U.S. 721, 731 (2003) (stereotype that "women's family duties trump those of the workplace" is a "gender stereotype"). L. Camille Hébert, *The Disparate Impact of Sexual Harassment: Does Motive Matter?,* 53 U. KAN. L. REV. 341, 342 (2005) (lower federal courts generally appear to have less difficulty with the question of whether the harassment was based on sex, at least in cases in which there was fairly strong evidence that the harassment was motivated by either sexual desire or gender-based animus).

8. Lea B. Vaughn, T*he Customer Is Always Right . . . Not! Employer Liability For Third Party Sexual Harassment,* 9 MICH. J. GENDER & L. 1, 7 (2002) (61.5% of the 553 women litigators surveyed reported being sexually harassed by clients in the last five years).

harassment.[9] Of course, whether certain conduct is serious enough to constitute legally actionable discrimination is sometimes uncertain. But survey responses and recent cases often reveal unquestionably abusive conduct, including sexual propositions, lewd

---

9. ABA Commission on Women in the Profession, The Unfinished Agenda: Women and the Legal Profession 18-19 (2001); Audrey Wolfson Latourette, *Sex Discrimination in the Legal Profession: Historical and Contemporary Perspectives,* 39 Val. U. L. Rev. 859, 894 (2005); Martha Neil, *Hidden Harassment: Law Firms and Disciplinary Authorities Look For Ways to Fight Sexual Misconduct,* 92 A.B.A. J. 43 (2006); *Are Women More Ethical Lawyers? An Empirical Study,* 31 Fla. St. U. L. Rev. 785, 837 (2004) ("Female lawyers around the country report a significant incidence of gender-based discrimination and incivility against them by judges, court personnel, other lawyers, and clients."); Lorraine Dusky, *Still Unequal: The Shameful Truth About Women and Justice in America* 223-24 (1996) (half of female litigators, 43% of law firm lawyers); Lynn S. Glasser, *Survey of Female Litigators: Discrimination by Clients Limits Opportunities, in* The Woman Advocate: Excelling in the '90s (Jean MacLean Snyder & Andra Barmash Greene eds. 1995) (55% of woman litigators reported harassment); Lisa Pfenninger, *Sexual Harassment in the Legal Profession: Workplace Education and Reform, Civil Remedies, and Professional Discipline,* 22 Fla. St. U. L. Rev. 171, 176-77 (1994) (citing surveys); Weidlich & Laurence, *supra* note 2 (51% of female lawyer respondents reported that they had experienced sexual harassment on the job); David N. Laband & Bernard F. Lentz, *Effects of Sexual Harassment on Job Satisfaction, Earnings, and Turnover Among Female Lawyers*, 51 Industrial & Labor Related Rev. 594 (1998) (66% of women in law firms and 46% of women in corporate and public sector organizations); Catherine E. Shanelaris et al., *Ten-Year Gender Survey*, New Hampshire B. J., March 1998, at 56-78 (between half and two-thirds of female lawyers in New Hampshire reported sexual harassment); Richard C. Kearney & Holley Taylor Sellers, *Gender Bias in Court Personnel Administration*, 81 Judicature 8 (1997) (49% of female court employees in Missouri reported instances of sexual advances to obtain job benefits; 35-40% of Rhode Island women experienced sexual comments, touching or disrespectful interest; 27% of Mississippi women experienced unwanted verbal or physical harassment); Myra C. Selby, *Examining Race and Gender Bias in the Courts: A Legacy of Indifference or Opportunity*, 32 Ind. L. Rev. 1167, 1172–73 (1999). *See also* Joan Brockman, Gender in the Legal Profession 115-19 (2001) (34% of surveyed Canadian women lawyers reported sexual harassment by lawyers, 12% by judges, and 10% by clients).

Of course, such surveys, based on subjective perceptions, do not necessarily indicate how much of the conduct labeled harassment would be sufficiently severe or pervasive to be legally actionable. For general problems in survey methodology, see Margaret A. Crouch, Thinking About Sexual Harassment: A Guide for the Perplexed 102-07 (2001).

comments, and groping.[10] Although systematic surveys of sexual harassment in law schools are lacking, reported incidents leave no doubt that a significant problem persists there as well. Many institutions have experienced racist, sexist, and homophobic comments in e-mails, graffiti, or anonymous flyers, and some have experienced even more egregious forms of sexual harassment by professors and peers.[11] In Law School Admission Council surveys, some form of discrimination is reported by about two-thirds of gay and lesbian students, a majority of African-American students, and a third of women, Asian-American, and Hispanic students.[12]

---

10. E.E.O.C. v. Rappaport, Hertz, Cherson & Rosenthal, P.C., 2006 WL 2660981 (E.D.N.Y. 2006) (EEOC filed suit against law firm in August 2005, claiming the firm violated federal antidiscrimination law and a 2003 consent decree in another case by failing to stop the sexual harassment of former firm employee. EEOC claimed harassment became so severe that former employee was forced to quit.). Woods v. Chubb & Son, 2005 WL 3271486 (9th Cir. 2005). Mellino v. Kampinski Co., L.P.A., 837 N.E.2d 385, 389 (Ohio App. 2005) (sexual harassment allegations made by the law firm's receptionist). Cincinnati Bar Assn. v. Young, 731 N.E. 2d 631 (Ohio, 2000); Wynn v. Mass. Comm'n Against Discrimination, 729 N.E.2d 1068 (Mass. 2000); Weeks v. Baker & McKenzie, 74 Cal. Rptr. 2d 510 (1st App. Dist. 1998); Rochester v. Fishman & Merrier, 1997 W L 24720 (1997) People v. Lowery, 894 P. 2d 758 (Colo. 1995); Reed Abelson, *By the Water Cooler in Cyberspace, the Talk Turns Ugly*, N.Y. TIMES, April 29, 2001, at A4, 24; Bill Kisliuk, *A Tale of Destruction*, SAN FRANCISCO RECORDER, March 5, 1997, at 1; Pfenninger, *supra* note 9, at 176-77, 179-80, 212; Grossman, *supra* note 4; Paul Braverman, *Manhandled,* AM. LAW., Aug. 2002, 73; *Hot Catalog, Hot Judge,* NAT'L L. J., April 22, 2002, at A13; COMMISSION ON WOMEN IN THE PROFESSION, VISIBLE INVISIBILITY: WOMEN OF COLOR IN LAW FIRMS 10-11 (2006).

11. Lisa G. Lerman, *Misconduct by Law Professors: Why It Matters*, 2004 PROF. LAW. 21, 26 (2004); Debra Baker, *Plague in the Profession*, A.B.A. J. 40-41 (September 2000); ABA COMMISSION ON WOMEN IN THE PROFESSION, ELUSIVE EQUALITY, THE EXPERIENCE OF WOMEN IN LEGAL EDUCATION 14-15, 25 (1996); Deborah L. Rhode, *Whistling Vivaldi: Legal Education and the Politics of Progress*, 23 N.Y.U. REV. LAW & SOCIAL CHANGE 217 (1997); Jennifer M. Russell, *On Being a Gorilla in Your Midst, or The Life of One Blackwoman in the Legal Academy,* 28 HARV. C. R.-C. L. L. REV. 259 (1993); *5 Women Leave FSU Faculty; Four of the Professors Said They Were Subjected to Constant Harassment and that Administrators "Turned a Blind Eye,"* ORLANDO SENTINEL, May 8, 1999, at D1.

12. Law School Outreach Project of the Chicago Bar Association Alliance for Women, Women Students' Experience of Gender Bias at Chicago Area Law Schools, vii, 27, 35, 56 (1995); LANI GUINIER, MICHELLE FINE & JANE BALIN, BECOMING GENTLEMEN, at 56, 28-29, 68 (1997); Rhode, *supra* note 11,

Although women are not the only victims of sex-based harassment, most complaints are brought by women. Figures specific to the legal profession are unavailable, but women initiate about 85% of all sexual harassment complaints filed with the federal Equal Employment Opportunity Commission.[13] Indeed, the number of sexual harassment claims filed with the EEOC increased by 20.38% from 1992 to 2005, with increases in the number of charges filed by women of every race and national origin.[14]

Moreover, retaliation—i.e., discharge, demotion, threats, reprimands, or other adverse action taken by employers to punish workers for reporting harassment and other forms of discrimination—remains a serious problem in the workplace. The number of retaliation complaints filed with the EEOC doubled from 1992 to 2005, with retaliation cases now making up nearly 30% of the EEOC's charge inventory.[15]

---

at 220; Dusky, *supra* note 9, at 28-39; Scott N. Ihrig, *Sexual Orientation in Law School: Experiences of Gay, Lesbian, and Bisexual Law Students*, 14 LAW AND INEQUALITY 555, 568 (1996); Janice L. Austin et al., *Results from a Survey: Gay, Lesbian, and Bisexual Students' Attitudes About Law School*, 48 J. LEGAL EDUC. 157, 166 (1998); Kim Brooks & Debra Parkes, *Queering Legal Education: A Project of Theoretical Discovery*, 27 HARV. WOMEN'S L.J. 89, 94 (2004) ("In one article, University of Minnesota law student Scott Ihrig describes how it felt to discuss *Bowers v. Hardwick* in his first-year constitutional law class.").

13. NATIONAL PARTNERSHIP FOR WOMEN & FAMILIES, WOMEN AT WORK: LOOKING BEHIND THE NUMBERS FORTY YEARS AFTER TITLE VII OF THE CIVIL RIGHTS ACT OF 1964 6 (2004).

14. *Id.* at 6. The National Partnership for Women & Families' 2004 analysis of EEOC data found that the number of sexual harassment claims filed by white women increased by 5% during the period 1992-2003, while the number of claims filed by African-American women over the same period increased by 42%, the number filed by Hispanic women increased by 120%, the number filed by Asian and Pacific Islander women increased by 100%, and the number filed by American Indian/Alaskan Native women increased by 114%. *Id.* at 6. As that study concluded: "These numbers indicate that sexual harassment remains a problem for all women workers. But, as with sex discrimination more broadly, racial and ethnic differences may make it more likely that some women will experience sexual harassment and file claims. The increases in claims filed by women of color may signal unique problems they face in the workforce, or a growing awareness of the remedies available to them when sexual harassment does occur." *Id.*

15. *Id.* at 12. *Sex Discrimination Cases Predominate in Recent Class Actions Filed by EEOC*, 71 U.S.L.W. 2158 (Sept. 10, 2002) (reporting that, of the 52 class action cases filed by the EEOC between Oct. 1, 2001 and June 30,

B. The Causes and Costs of Sex-Based Harassment

The causes of sex-based harassment are complex and contested.[16] Most experts believe that sexual harassment is more often about power than about sex. Harassing conduct reflects and reinforces gender stereotypes and gender subordination: it often functions as a means of preserving male status, control, and dominance.[17] Individuals who view demeaning or sexually explicit comments as isolated, inadvertent, and relatively harmless banter may feel that women who complain are overreacting and that they should just "grow up and stop whining."[18] But such incidents need to be seen as

---

2002, 25 of the cases included claims of retaliation). Retaliation carries especially great potential for harm because it deters victims from reporting harassment.

16. Theresa M. Beiner, *Let the Jury Decide: The Gap Between What Judges and Reasonable People Believe Is Sexually Harassing,* 75 S. CAL. L. REV. 791, 791 (2002) (human resources professionals say biggest problem they have with sexual harassment is that employees do not know what behaviors constitute sexual harassment); Caroline Forell, *The Meaning of Equality: Sexual Harassment, Stalking, and Provocation in Canada, Australia, and the United States*, 28 T. JEFFERSON L. REV. 151, 151 (2005) ("When men and women are compared, formal equality usually means that women's conduct is measured against a male norm.").

17. Vickie Schultz, *Reconceptualizing Sexual Harassment,* 107 YALE L. J. 1683, 1755-61 (1998); Kathryn Abrams, *The New Jurisprudence of Sexual Harassment*, 83 CORNELL L. REV. 1169, 1205-13 (1998); Katherine M. Franke, *What's Wrong with Sexual Harassment?*, 49 STAN. L. REV. 691, 696 (1997); Andrea Meryl Kirshenbaum, *Because of... Sex: Rethinking the Protections Afforded Under Title VII in the Post-Oncale World*, 69 ALB. L. REV. 139, 177 (2006). Valorie L. Vojdik, *Beyond Stereotyping in Equal Protection Doctrine: Reframing the Exclusion of Women from Combat*, 57 ALA. L. REV. 303, 305 (2005) (discusses sexual harassment as a means of devaluing and subordinating women in workplace); Susan P. Stuart, *Jack and Jill Go to Court: Litigating a Peer Sexual Harassment Case Under Title IX*, 29 AM. J. TRIAL ADVOC. 243, 296 (2005) (harassment cases really are more about gender discrimination than about sex); Robert A. Kearney, *The Unintended Hostile Environment: Mapping the Limits of Sexual Harassment Law*, 25 BERKELEY J. EMP. & LAB. L. 87, 127 (2004) (noting Franke's argument that "sexual harassment is sex discrimination precisely because its use and effect police hetero-patriarchal gender norms in the workplace").

18. State Bar of Texas, Gender Bias Task Force of Texas, Final Report 20, 25 (1994); Diane F. Norwood & Arlette Molling, *Sex Discrimination in the Profession*, TEXAS BUS. J., June 1992 at 50, 51; Deborah L. Rhode, *Gender and the Profession: The No-Problem Problem*, 30 HOFSTRA L. REV. 1001,

part of a larger pattern that undermines women's authority, confidence, competence, and credibility.[19] Women want to be treated as professionals, not as sexual objects.[20]

The price of sex-based harassment is substantial, both for individuals who are targets and for the organizations that employ them. For victims, harassment often results in economic and psychological injuries, such as loss of employment opportunities, unwanted transfers, anxiety, depression, and other stress-related conditions.[21] Organizations pay the price in decreased productivity, increased turnover, impaired recruitment, and greater risks of legal liability.[22]

1002 (2002) ("if women will just 'concentrate on the job and get the chip off their shoulders . . . they should do fine in today's society'"; and "[o]f all the problems we have as lawyers . . . discrimination is low on the list of important ones").

19. ABA COMMISSION ON WOMEN, *supra* note 9, at 21; Diane Gentry, *Title VII Limitations—Keeping the Workplace Hostile,* 9 CARDOZO WOMEN'S L.J. 393, 393 (2003) ("Although harassment can be communicated through sexual content, much harassment is motivated exclusively by gender animosity. Such forms of harassment include "characterizing the work as appropriate for men only; denigrating women's performance or ability to master the job; providing patronizing forms of help in performing the job . . . denying . . . deserved promotions, [and] isolating women from the social networks that confer a sense of belonging.").

20. *See* sources cited in KATHARINE T. BARTLETT, ANGELA P. HARRIS & DEBORAH L. RHODE, GENDER AND LAW: THEORY, DOCTRINE, COMMENTARY (3d ed. 2002); Brockman, *supra* note 9, at 11-20; Rhode, *supra* note 18, at 100; Crouch, *supra* note 9, at 131. The differences in male/female perceptions should not be overstated. *Id*., at 128-32. Of course, women can be harassers, too; legal professionals of both genders must take care not to engage in abusive behavior.

21. KERRY SEAGRAVE, THE SEXUAL HARASSMENT OF WOMEN IN THE WORKPLACE: 1600 TO 1993, 203 (1994); Laband & Lentz, *supra* note 9, at 600-04; L. Camille Hebert, *The Disparate Impact of Sexual Harassment: Does Motive Matter?* 53 U. KAN. L. REV. 341, 387-388 (2005) (empirical evidence suggests that women are more likely than men to suffer significant negative personal and work consequences as the result of sexually harassing conduct); Audrey Wolfson Latourette, *Sex Discrimination in the Legal Profession: Historical and Contemporary Perspectives*, 39 VAL. U. L. REV. 859, 894 (2005) (". . . inequities do exist despite the popular belief that women are no longer discriminated against in the legal profession. . . . The facts show that the odds of a woman being made partner are less than one-third of the odds for a man being named partner.").

22. Deborah Rhode, *Access to Justice*, 40 HARV. C.R.-C.L. L. REV. 559, 559-60 (2005) (citing Seagrave at 203, noting "Sexual harassment lawsuits, for instance, were once regarded as unnecessary and frivolous—the 'petty slights of the hypersensitive'—until studies revealed that the average *Fortune*

These risks can be considerable, in terms of reputation as well as dollars.

One early publicized example involved a multimillion-dollar verdict against a San Francisco law firm for its failure to take seriously a top rainmaker's six-year pattern of harassment of a legal secretary and other employees.[23] The jury's verdict included $50,000 in compensatory damages assessed against both the firm and the partner, $225,000 in punitive damages against the partner, and $6.9 million (later reduced to $3.5 million) in punitive damages against the firm.[24] The public relations and related costs to the firm were even greater, particularly when its mishandling of the complaint became a cover story for *American Lawyer*.[25]

Egregious harassment can also subject lawyers to disciplinary action under state bar rules of professional conduct, including those that ban gender bias and/or conduct reflecting adversely on one's fitness to practice law.[26] In 2005, for example, the Delaware Supreme Court upheld the three-year suspension of a lawyer who had engaged in repeated verbal and physical harassment of clients and employees. *In re Tenenbaum*, 880 A.2d 1025 (Del. 2005). In *Cincinnati Bar Association v. Young*, 731 N.E.2d 631 (Ohio 2000), the Ohio Supreme Court affirmed a two-year suspension for a lawyer who made sexually explicit comments and propositions to a law student under his supervision, and who engaged in verbal and physi-

---

500 company lost approximately six million dollars in turnover, worker absences, and lost productivity as a result of these apparently insignificant injuries."). Laband & Lentz, *supra* note 9, at 600-04; Seagrave, *supra* note 21, at 203-04.

23. Jane Gross, *When the Biggest Firm Faces Sexual Harassment Suit*, N.Y. TIMES, July 29, 1994, at B7.

24. Martha Neil, *Hidden Harassment*, A.B.A. J., March 1, 2006; Reynolds Holding, *The Case that Changed the Workplace*, S. F. CHRON., Oct. 15, 2000, at 3.

25. *See also* Sier v. Jacobs, Persinger & Parker, 276 A.D. 2d 401 (N.Y. App. 2000), in which a jury awarded $250,000 for emotional distress and $50,000 in punitive damages.

26. ABA Commission on Women, *supra* note 9, at 48 n.307. For specific provisions *see, e.g.*, MINN. RULES OF PROF'L CONDUCT, R. 8.4, and CAL. RULES OF PROF'L CONDUCT, R. 2-400; ILL. RULES OF PROF'L CONDUCT, R. 8.4(a)(5); Pfenninger, *supra* note 9, at 212, 214. For anti-bias provisions *see, e.g.*, OHIO CODE OF PROF'L RESPONSIBILITY 1-102(B); N. J. RULES OF PROF'L CONDUCT, R. 8.4(g). For conduct adversely affecting fitness to practice, *see* ABA, MODEL CODE OF PROF'L RESPONSIBILITY DR 1-102(A)(6); ABA, MODEL RULES OF PROF. CONDUCT R. 8.4(d).

cal abuse toward legal assistants and secretaries (the second year of the suspension was stayed pending the attorney's successful completion of a civility course). Similarly, in *In re White*, 611 S.E.2d 917 (S.C. 2005), the Supreme Court of South Carolina affirmed an 18-month suspension of a lawyer who had multiple violations of attorney discipline rules, including violations based on his sexual harassment of a client.

C. Sex-Based Harassment and the Law

Sex-based harassment is prohibited as a form of sex discrimination in the workplace by federal law (if the employer has more than 15 employees and/or if the employer is an educational institution that receives federal funds) and by the laws of many states and municipalities (many states cover even smaller employers; Illinois' statutory prohibition on harassment, for example, covers employers of one or more employees). Employers may also face liability for sex-based harassment under state tort and contract law for claims such as assault, negligent retention, wrongful discharge, and intentional interference with contractual relations. Remedies can include back pay, front pay, compensation for emotional distress, punitive damages, and attorney's fees.

In 1980, the EEOC issued authoritative guidelines on sexual harassment under Title VII of the Civil Rights Act of 1964, imposing on employers "an affirmative duty" to prevent and eliminate sexual abuse.[27] The guidelines define sexual harassment as follows:

> Unwanted sexual advances, requests for sexual favors, and other verbal or physical conduct of a sexual nature constitute sexual harassment when any one of three criteria is met: (1) Submission to such conduct is made either explicitly or implicitly a term or condition of the individual's employment. (2) Submission to or rejection of such conduct by an individual is used as the basis for employment decisions affecting such individual. (3) Such conduct has the purpose or effect of unreasonably interfering with an individual's work performance or creating an intimidating, hostile, or offensive work environment. 29 C.F.R. § 1604.11(a).

---

27. 42 U.S.C. 2000e-2a, 29 C.F.R. §1604.11.

The EEOC later made clear that "harassment not involving sexual activity or language may also give rise to Title VII liability . . . if it is 'sufficiently patterned or pervasive' and directed at employees because of their sex[28] and that an employer may be vicariously liable for harassment."[29]

Several United States Supreme Court cases have clarified the law concerning sex-based harassment. *Meritor Savings Bank v. Vinson*, 477 U.S. 57 (1986), confirmed that sex-based harassment is a form of illegal sex discrimination, actionable under Title VII of the Civil Rights Act of 1964. The Court interpreted Title VII's language prohibiting discrimination in the "terms, conditions, or privileges of employment" as covering the psychological, as well as financial, aspects of employment. The Court held that Title VII gives "employees the right to work in an environment free from discriminatory intimidation, ridicule, and insult," even where tangible employment benefits such as pay and promotion are not affected. *Id.* at 65.

Seven years later, in *Harris v. Forklift Systems, Inc.*, 510 U.S. 17 (1993), the Supreme Court again focused on harassment that creates a hostile work environment. In *Harris*, the Court held that conduct need not seriously affect a complainant's psychological well-being to be actionable. Rather, hostile work environment harassment violates Title VII as long as it is both subjectively offensive to the complainant and objectively offensive to "a reasonable person." *Id.* at 21. Factors that are relevant in determining whether an environment is hostile or abusive include: "the frequency of the conduct; its severity; whether it is physically threatening or humiliating, or a mere offensive utterance; and whether it unreasonably interferes with an employee's work performance." *Id.* at 23.

In 1998, in *Oncale v. Sundowner Offshore Services, Inc.*, 523 U.S. 75 (1998), the Court held that same-sex harassment—i.e., harassment of a man by a man, or harassment of a woman by a woman—can be actionable under Title VII.

That same year, in *Faragher v. City of Boca Raton*, 524 U.S. 775 (1998) and *Burlington Industries v. Ellerth*, 524 U.S. 742 (1998), the Court clarified the circumstances under which employers will be held liable for harassment committed by their agents and em-

28. EEOC, Policy Guidance on Sexual Harassment (March 19, 1990).

29. Enforcement Guidance: Vicarious Employer Liability for Unlawful Harassment by Supervisors (June 1999).

ployees. *Faragher* involved a female lifeguard's claims that her male supervisors had harassed her in a variety of ways, including offensive touching and lewd and derogatory comments about women. *Id.* at 780. The Supreme Court created the following framework for assessing such claims:

> An employer is subject to vicarious liability to a victimized employee for an actionable hostile environment created by a supervisor with immediate (or successively higher) authority over the employee. When no tangible employment action is taken, a defending employer may raise an affirmative defense to liability or damages, subject to proof by a preponderance of the evidence. The defense comprises two necessary elements: (a) that the employer exercised reasonable care to prevent and correct promptly any sexually harassing behavior, and (b) that the plaintiff employee unreasonably failed to take advantage of any preventive or corrective opportunities provided by the employer or to avoid harm otherwise. While proof that an employer had promulgated an antiharassment policy with a complaint procedure is not necessary in every instance as a matter of law, the need for a stated policy suitable to the employment circumstances may appropriately be addressed in any case when litigating the first element of the defense. And while proof that an employee failed to fulfill the corresponding obligation of reasonable care to avoid harm is not limited to showing an unreasonable failure to use any complaint procedure provided by the employer, a demonstration of such failure will normally suffice to satisfy the employer's burden under the second element of the defense. No affirmative defense is available, however, when the supervisor's harassment culminates in a tangible employment action, such as discharge, demotion, or undesirable assignment. . . .

Id. at 807-08.

The Court concluded that the employer had failed to establish this affirmative defense. The employer's sexual harassment policy had not been distributed to the plaintiff or to her supervisors. Nor did the policy "include any assurance that the harassing supervisors could be bypassed in registering complaints." For these reasons, the Court found that the employer had not exercised reasonable care to prevent and correct harassment. *Id.* at 808-09.

In *Burlington Industries v. Ellerth*, 524 U.S. 742 (1998), the plaintiff alleged that she had been subject to constant sexual harassment by one of her supervisors, who threatened to make her life difficult but did not take any specific adverse employment action against her; the plaintiff had not complained to anyone in authority. The Court reiterated the principles set forth in *Faragher*, which automatically impose liability upon employers for tangible employment actions taken by their supervisors, while providing the opportunity for an affirmative defense when supervisors create a hostile work environment that does not involve a tangible employment action. Under the Court's definition, a "tangible employment action constitutes a significant change in employment status, such as hiring, firing, failing to promote, reassignment with significantly different responsibilities, or a decision causing a significant change in benefits." *Id.* at 761. Because a tangible employment decision requires an "official act of the enterprise . . . [it] becomes for Title VII purposes, the act of the employer," which is sufficient to justify liability. The Court found that the plaintiff had not alleged that she had suffered a tangible employment action, but remanded the case to allow the plaintiff to amend her pleading or supplement her discovery and to allow the employer to assert and prove any affirmative defense.

Faragher and *Ellerth* did not resolve all issues involving employer liability. Questions remain about whether particular conduct is gender-based or whether it is sufficiently severe or pervasive to be actionable as sexual harassment. Although most successful claims involve conduct that is sexually charged, any abusive behaviors that are directed at individuals on the basis of sex can result in liability.[30] In some contexts, it may be difficult to determine whether the employer took reasonable care to prevent and correct harassment, or whether the plaintiff acted unreasonably in failing to avoid harm. State and local laws may also be relevant in resolving these questions. Such complexities underscore the need for explicit policies and educational programs designed to minimize the chances for misunderstanding about what constitutes harassment.

Title VII also prohibits employers from retaliating against employees for reporting harassment (or other types of illegal discrimina-

---

30. *See e.g.,* Smith v. First Union Nat'l Bank, 202 F.3d 234 (4th Cir. 2000); Easko v. Howard County, Md., 2005 U.S. Dist. LEXIS 37602 (D. Md. 2005).

tion) or for filing a charge, testifying, assisting, or participating in Title VII investigations, proceedings, or hearings. 42 U.S.C. § 2000e-3. As the Supreme Court recently made clear in *Burlington Northern & Santa Fe Railway Co. v. White*, 126 S. Ct. 2405 (2006), an employer violates Title VII's anti-retaliation protections when it takes action against an employee that would be considered materially adverse by a reasonable employee—i.e., when an employer takes retaliatory actions that "could well dissuade a reasonable worker from making or supporting a charge of discrimination." In that particular case, the Court found that the employer had committed illegal retaliation by assigning an employee who had complained of sex discrimination to a job with less desirable duties. *Id.* at 2416-18. The Court also found that indefinitely suspending the employee without pay—even though the employee eventually received her pay—would likely deter a reasonable employee from reporting discrimination and thus also constituted illegal retaliation. *Id.* Indeed, the Court made clear that Title VII's antiretaliation protections are even broader than the statute's other antidiscrimination provisions, "extend[ing] beyond workplace-related or employment-related retaliatory acts and harm." *Id.* at 2414. Moreover, workers who make good-faith reports of sexual harassment are protected from retaliation even if it turns out that the behavior at issue did not constitute illegal harassment.[31]

D. The Importance of Sex-Based Harassment Policies, Remedies, and Preventive Programs

Policies that promote awareness, provide adequate complaint channels, and ensure effective responses can decrease the likelihood of harassment and all its costs by making every employee aware of the rules. In addition to promoting a professional work environment—thus preventing harassment before it happens—written anti-harassment policies can support an employer's affirmative defense to liability if harassment does occur.

The *Faragher*, *Ellerth*, and *Burlington Northern* rulings underscore the need for adequate policies and practices concerning sex-

31. *See, e.g.*, Pryor v. Seyfarth, Shaw, Fairweather & Geraldson, 212 F.3d 976 (7th Cir. 2000) (granting summary judgment to defendant law firm on plaintiff secretary's sexual harassment claim but allowing her retaliation claim to continue).

based harassment. Such initiatives are crucial for all legal employers, including large and small firms, law schools, government entities, and nonprofit organizations.[32] Of course, because legal employers vary in structure, size, and scope, no "one size fits all" policy is appropriate. An employer must tailor its approach to fit its particular needs and to reflect current federal, state, and local law. This manual identifies a range of practices that merit consideration as each legal employer crafts its own policy.

Key elements of effective policies include antiretaliation protections and complaint channels that are responsive to the concerns of all affected parties. A wide array of research finds that only a small minority of those who experience harassment, typically between 5 and 10 percent, make any formal complaint, and that fewer still pursue legal remedies.[33] For most individuals, the expense, embarrassment, and evidentiary hurdles associated with bringing a sexual harassment claim are sufficient to deter formal proceedings.

Many employees also fear that the risks of retaliation and stigma will outweigh the likelihood of an effective response. Those fears are not unsubstantiated. In one representative survey, a third of women who complained about harassment believed that their action made the situation worse, and only a fifth believed that their complaints were treated fairly; another study found that nearly half of women who report harassment later experience some sort of retaliation on the job.[34]

---

32. Anna Marie Kukec, *Tightening the Gaps Is Key for Management,* BAR LEADER, Aug. 1997, at 40 (reporting that only 44% of surveyed bar associations had sexual harassment policies).

33. *See* sources cited in Rhode, *supra* note 18 at 99; Margaret Moore Jackson, *A Different Voicing of Unwelcomeness: Relational Reasoning and Sexual Harassment,* 81 N.D.L.R. 739 (2005); Deborah Zalesne, *Sexual Harassment Law: Has It Gone Too Far or Has the Media?*, 8 TEMPLE POL. & CIVIL R. L. REV. 351, 367 (1999); Louise E. Fitzgerald, Suzanne Swan & Karen Fisher, *Why Didn't She Just Report Him?: The Psychological and Legal Implications of Women's Responses to Sexual Harassment*, 51 J. SOC. ISSUES 117 (1995); U.S. MERIT SYSTEMS PROTECTION BOARD, SEXUAL HARASSMENT IN THE FEDERAL WORKPLACE 30, 33 (1995) (finding that only 6% of workers who reported being sexually harassed took formal action and only 12% informally reported the harassment to a supervisor).

34. Ann C. Wendt & William M. Slonaker, *Sexual Harassment and Retaliation: A Double-Edged Sword*, SAM (Society for Advancement of Management) ADVANCED MGMT. J. 56 (Autumn 2002); *see also* Deborah Brake,

Those who immediately report harassment run the risk of being labeled oversensitive, vindictive, or "whiny." By contrast, those who hold back on reporting in the hope that the conduct will not be repeated might undermine their own credibility and prevent an effective response; employees who anticipate such reactions may never complain.[35] To counter these obstacles to reporting, employers should do whatever they can to preserve confidentiality and to prevent retaliation.

By the same token, an effective policy on sex-based harassment must ensure that the complaint process is fair, and appears fair, to those accused of misconduct. Some men express reluctance to mentor or travel with women out of fear of unjust accusations of harassment or the appearance of a sexual relationship.[36] A lack of confidence in workplace complaint procedures is likely to exacerbate such concerns.

While this manual focuses on sex-based harassment, harassment on the basis of race, national origin, religion, disability, age, and sexual orientation also creates barriers to equal employment opportunity and imposes a range of costs upon employers, including decreased morale and performance. Moreover, such harassment may be prohibited by federal and/or state and local antidiscrimination law, as well as by state bar ethics codes. For all these reasons, legal employers should address these issues as well—either in separate policies or as part of a comprehensive anti-harassment policy.

Retaliation, 90 MINN. L. REV. 18, 32-36 (2005) (discussing studies in which women and people of color who reported discrimination suffered more negative consequences than the men and whites who reported discrimination); Fitzgerald, Swan & Fisher, *supra* note 33. For discussion of the disincentives to report harassment, *see* BROCKMAN, *supra* note 9, at 133; Katherine Kim, *A Feminist Critique: The Term Sexual Harassment Once Packed a Wallop, But for 20-Something Women Today, It's Almost a Joke*, 151 N.J. L.J. 1367 (1998); Weidlich & Lawrence, *supra* note 2; Laura Gatland, *Sexual Harassment: An Ounce of Prevention*, PERSPECTIVES, Fall 1998, at 4.

35. Bartlett, Harris & Rhode, *supra* note 20; Rhode, *supra* note 18, at 101; Susan Estrich, *Sex at Work*, 43 STAN. L. REV. 826-34, 843-47 (1991).

36. ABA COMMISSION ON WOMEN, *supra* note 7, at 20; Cynthia Fuchs Epstein, et al., *Glass Ceilings and Open Doors: Women's Advancement in the Legal Profession*," 64 FORDHAM L. REV. 291, 356 (1995).

PART **II**

FORMULATING AND IMPLEMENTING HARASSMENT POLICIES

A. Drafting and Revising a Policy

It is generally desirable for organizations to have a specific committee that is responsible for formulating and evaluating a policy on sex-based harassment. The membership of such a committee should be diverse in terms of sex, race, ethnicity, age, seniority, sexual orientation, and related characteristics. Where possible, it should include individuals with expertise in discrimination law and members of the support staff as well as attorneys. Most important, members of the committee should be individuals who are widely respected, who appreciate the importance of the issues to be addressed, and who will lend credibility to the process. Committee members should familiarize themselves with relevant law and organizational practices. A process should be established for consultation and/or training with those who are affected by the policy, as well as others outside the organization who have confronted such issues.

B. Communicating and Implementing the Policy

The initial draft of a policy or major modifications in its content should be circulated for comment and revised accordingly. Once a final version is adopted, it should be disseminated, and employees should acknowledge in writing that they have received it.

Some jurisdictions require that employers reissue and train employees in the policy annually.[1] Many organizations do so voluntarily.[2] Best practices would suggest training and refresher training on a regular basis. A covering memorandum should emphasize strong support for the policy from those in managerial positions. The drafting committee should also ensure that information about the policy is included in training and orientation materials as well as in any organizational handbooks or related publications. The policy should be posted on the employer's intranet and in locations in the workplace, including remote locations, that employees at all levels frequent regularly. The manner in which a policy is presented is crucial to its reception and support.

C. Reviewing the Policy

A designated committee should periodically review the harassment policy. Such reviews should take place after there has been a reasonable time period to evaluate the policy in its initial phase or after any material change in its contents or in the relevant law. The goal of these reviews should be to determine whether the policy has been effectively implemented and whether revisions are necessary. In conducting these evaluations, committee members should find ways to assess the experience of those who have been subject to the policy, whether as complainants, alleged harassers, witnesses, investigators, or administrators.

1. For example, California requires that employers with 50 or more employees mandate sexual harassment training every two years for its California-based supervisors. Cal. Gov't Code § 12950.1.

2. Moreover, many employment liability insurers verify annually that their policyholders conduct regular training on the policy.

PART III

ESSENTIAL ELEMENTS OF A POLICY ON SEX-BASED HARASSMENT

A comprehensive policy on sex-based harassment should seek to prevent such conduct and ensure an appropriate response. To that end, the policy should clearly define the kinds of behavior that will not be tolerated and state the sanctions that will be imposed if this behavior occurs.

A comprehensive sex-based harassment policy should include:

- A strong statement of the organization's unwillingness to tolerate sex-based harassment;
- A statement specifying that employees who complain of sex-based harassment will be protected from retaliation;
- A clearly articulated definition of sex-based harassment, with examples of inappropriate behavior;
- Identification of individuals covered under the policy;
- Multiple avenues for filing a complaint;
- Procedures to be followed in response to sex-based harassment complaints that afford the maximum feasible confidentiality and protection from retaliation and unwarranted accusations;
- A commitment to respond promptly to known harassment whether or not a formal complaint is made;
- A specification of possible sanctions;
- Explanation of the appeals process, if any;
- A mechanism for implementing and monitoring the policy; and
- Educational and training programs, including refresher training.

Employers should also periodically review their policies to ensure compliance with applicable federal, state, and local law.

A. Policy Statement

The introduction to the policy should make clear that sex-based harassment will not be tolerated. For example:

> The Association maintains a long-standing commitment against any form of sexual harassment in the work environment in keeping with published guidelines of the Equal Employment Opportunity Commission. This policy applies without exception. After an investigation, employees who are found to have engaged in sexual harassment will be subject to disciplinary sanctions including suspension, demotion or involuntary termination;[1] or

The firm is committed to maintaining a professional work environment that is free of bias, prejudice, or harassment. Sex-based harassment is illegal and will not be tolerated in the office, at work assignments outside the office, at office-sponsored social functions, or in any context subject to the firm's control (see Appendix I).

B. Definition of Sex-Based Harassment

An effective policy also requires a clear, concise definition of sex-based harassment, which is illustrated by concrete examples of unacceptable behavior. Many legal employers use plain language to elaborate on the EEOC Guidelines and to express a strong commitment to eradicating gender bias. The most helpful policies provide examples of actionable sex-based harassment, such as:

- Demands for sexual favors in exchange for continued employment or favorable reviews, assignments, commendations, or promotions;
- Continued or repeated sexual jokes, epithets, advances, or propositions;
- Verbal abuse of a sexual nature or of a hostile nature directed at one sex;
- Graphic verbal commentary about sexual prowess, attractiveness, or deficiencies;
- Sexually degrading or vulgar descriptions of another individual;
- Leering, whistling, touching, pinching, or assaults;

1. ABA Personnel Policies & Practices Manual (revised 1/1/98).

- Suggestive, insulting, or obscene comments or gestures;
- Coercive sexual acts;
- Workplace displays of sexually suggestive objects, pictures, posters, graffiti, or cartoons;
- Questions about sexual conduct, sexual orientation, or sexual preferences;
- Hostile, demeaning, or intimidating conduct that is consistently targeted at only one sex, even if the content is not sexual;
- Electronic transmission or display of sexually explicit, demeaning, or hostile materials;
- Unwillingness to train, assist, or cooperate with a colleague on the basis of sex;
- Destruction or sabotage of work on the basis of sex; and
- Retaliation against employees for complaining about such behaviors.

C. Identification of Individuals Covered Under the Policy

A sex-based harassment policy must clearly identify those subject to its coverage. The best policies are all-inclusive; they cover students, employees, professors, support staff, paralegals, associates, and partners. Not only should current employees be included, but applicants, potential employees, and former employees as well. The policy should also cover non-employees, such as clients, vendors, or opposing counsel, even though employer liability for their conduct is unsettled. To ensure an environment of equal opportunity and respect, employers should encourage reporting of all incidents of harassment, regardless of whether the harasser is subject to the organization's direct control. Many legal employers and educational institutions have strategies for handling abusive conduct by others. For example, law schools can deny placement facilities to law firms whose members have engaged in sex-based harassment of a student. Law firms can direct the supervising or managing partner to address unacceptable behavior by a client.

D. Consensual Relationships

A troubling issue for many organizations is what to do about consensual relationships. Such relationships can pose problems on several levels. First, where the parties are in a supervisory/subordinate relationship, it may be difficult to determine whether the junior party is truly acting freely. Second, even if the relationship is fully consensual, other employers or students may perceive the fact or appearance of favoritism. Third, even relationships that begin as consensual may sour and create risks of retaliation or strained work environments. The vast majority of human resources personnel agree that workplace romances are dangerous because they can lead to legal liability or conflict within the organization.[2]

Yet deciding what steps an employer can take to prevent such difficulties is equally problematic. Most workplaces have no formal policies concerning romantic involvement, and only a small percentage ban them entirely.[3] Human resources experts express concerns that attempting to prohibit all consensual relationships will simply force them underground and impose the costs of secrecy with few offsetting benefits.[4] However, about four-fifths of surveyed human resources personnel also believe that such romantic involvement should be impermissible between supervisors and subordinates.[5] Some legal employers and law schools either ban or discourage intimate relationships between those in a supervisory/subordinate relationship. For example:

> The firm discourages consensual sexual or romantic relationships between individuals when one of the parties has any direct or indirect supervisory responsibility over the other. Parties who enter into such relationships should take prompt steps to terminate the supervisory responsibility.

---

2. Over four-fifths of surveyed personnel believed that workplace conflict could result from romantic involvements, and three-quarters were concerned about potential legal liability. Society for Human Resource Management, Workplace Romance Survey 3 (2002). *See also* SHRM 2006 Workplace Romance Survey; *Perceptions of Consensual Amorous Relationship Policies* (CARPS), Journal of College and Character, http://collegevalues.org/articles.cfm?a=1&id=1329 (2007).

3. In the most recent comprehensive survey, involving some 3,000 employers, less than 25% had written or verbal policy on workplace romances, and of those that did, only 9% banned them entirely. Society for Human Resource Management, 2006 survey, *supra* note 2, at 1-2.

4. Laura Gatland, *Sexual Harassment: An Ounce of Prevention*, Perspectives, Fall 1998, at 7; Deborah L. Rhode. *Danger or Delight? Is Romance at Work All Bad?*, Nat'l L. J. Nov. 23, 1998, at A21.

5. Society for Human Resources Management, *supra* note 35, at 6.

PART IV

RESPONSES TO COMPLAINTS OF SEX-BASED HARASSMENT

A. Reporting a Complaint

The policy should provide a clear course of conduct for individuals who experience sex-based harassment. Some policies encourage individuals to attempt to resolve the problem with the person directly responsible for it, either before or in conjunction with making an official complaint. At a minimum, it is appropriate for policies to underscore that individuals who believe they have been subject to harassment should indicate promptly and firmly to offenders that their behavior is unwelcome. Effective policies recognize, however, that disparities of power and status may sometimes deter any direct confrontation by those who experience harassment. The policy should not make such notice a prerequisite to a complaint.

The policy should set forth procedures for making a complaint. It is generally recommended that the policy designate multiple complaint channels. Several options are important because complainants may be uncomfortable approaching certain individuals about the situation. For example, the person who is designated to receive the complaint might also be responsible for the harassment.[1] Providing multiple complaint channels increases the likelihood that incidents of sex-based harassment will be reported and redressed.

---

1. In *Meritor Savings Bank v. Vinson*, 477 U.S. 57 (1986), the Supreme Court criticized the employer for having a grievance procedure that required the employee to complain to her supervisor, who was the alleged harasser. *Id.* at 73.

The individuals responsible for receiving complaints must be carefully selected and trained. They should be widely respected and committed to handling sensitive matters as carefully and confidentially as practical. If possible, they should include individuals of both sexes and different ages and seniority (e.g., supervisory staff member, a senior associate, a partner).

Employees should not be required to report sex-based harassment to their immediate supervisors. Even if the supervisor is not the target of the allegations, knowledge of the complaint could adversely affect workplace relationships. The policy may, however, give complainants the option to report to the supervisor in an effort to resolve the problem informally and discreetly. The policy should require supervisors who resolve such an incident to make a confidential report to the organization's management. Records should be kept in order to disclose any pattern of harassment by a particular individual. Incidents that do not appear serious in isolation assume broader significance when they reflect a continued course of conduct.

Well-drafted policies generally give complainants the option of making either an oral or written complaint of sex-based harassment and require that they receive notice of their legal rights and applicable deadlines for exercising them. An oral complaint should be immediately reduced to writing by the person receiving the report and submitted to the complainant for signed approval. Alternatively, a written complaint should describe the conduct at issue in the form of a confidential memorandum to anyone designated in the policy to receive complaints.

Individuals who know of sex-based harassment that is directed at other individuals should also be encouraged to report the misconduct. Some policies require reporting by those who believe another employee has been a victim of sex-based harassment; other policies state that those who have been told of such incidents should report them.

Complaint channels and reporting procedures may vary in accordance with the size of the organization and the position of involved parties. Employers should ensure that employees at remote locations and part-time employees have notice of the policy and have reasonable means to register complaints. Some policies distinguish between associates and partners or between lawyers and administrative staff.

In a small organization, the managing partner, general counsel, or department head may be the logical person to receive sex-based harassment complaints, unless, of course, he or she is the harasser. In that case, the next senior person might be designated to receive complaints. Larger organizations often create a specific position or committee structure for handling such issues. Whatever the structure, it is important to provide several reporting alternatives and to list the appropriate persons by name and title.

The report of a complaint should contain as much detail as possible regarding the offensive behavior. Accordingly, the firm policy should suggest that individuals who experience harassment keep a record of the objectionable conduct. It should, however, be noted that if complainants are unsatisfied with their organization's resolution of the issue and later file suit, a record kept at the direction of the employer's policy rather than in anticipation of litigation may not be privileged. Individuals might be forced to reveal notes they never thought would be made public. Therefore, the organization's policy, while encouraging the creation of a record, should put complainants on notice of this possible disclosure requirement and explain that only notes kept in anticipation of litigation are privileged.

In an attempt to handle sex-based harassment as quickly as possible, many policies require that complaints be made promptly. Although it is desirable to encourage timely reporting in order to take expeditious action, setting a rigid time frame ignores the way that individuals subject to sex-based harassment usually respond. Most hope the incident will not be repeated and fear retaliation or notoriety if they complain. Victims are often reluctant to file a complaint until repetition of the offensive behavior leaves them no choice. The policy should recognize that sex-based harassment can be a traumatic experience. Late reporting should not in and of itself preclude remedial action, particularly since it will not absolve the organization of its duty to address harassing conduct.

Individuals who make a complaint should receive information about the organization's procedures for prompt investigation and resolution of the matter. Complainants should be assured that the organization will address the matter to its best ability under the law while taking into consideration their preferences about any remedial action.

B. Protection Against Retaliation

An otherwise well-conceived policy may be ineffective if it does not provide adequate safeguards against retaliation. The absence of a statement on this subject can have a chilling effect on individuals' willingness to report. Accordingly, the policy should include a provision such as:

> The Company or Firm will not in any way retaliate against an employee, potential employee, or former employee who makes a report of discrimination or harassment.
>
> Retaliation against any individual for reporting sex-based harassment will not be tolerated and will be subject to the same strict sanctions as the harassment itself.
>
> Retaliation is a very serious violation of the law and of this policy and should be reported immediately.

Retaliation against a complainant, whether by the alleged harasser or by other individuals, is itself a form of sex-based harassment. Accordingly, it should subject offenders to the same disciplinary sanctions provided for other harassing conduct. If the original subject of a complaint engages in retaliation, the sanctions should be harsher than what would have been imposed for the initial sexual harassment alone. Individuals who are not themselves complainants but who assist in a sex-based harassment investigation should also be protected from retaliation under the policy. Once a complaint is made, personnel receiving or investigating complaints should remind all involved parties of the organization's retaliation policy and the legal remedies available to any individuals, including complainants and witnesses, who experience reprisals. All involved parties should be counseled to report any violations of the organization's retaliation policy.

C. Investigating a Complaint

Appropriate strategies for investigating complaints are a key part of any effective policy on sex-based harassment. Investigators should receive training, and the policy should provide guidance on issues such as confidentiality, procedural fairness, and interviewing techniques. Refresher training should be provided periodically.

1. Confidentiality

To the maximum extent possible, an investigatory process should protect the privacy of the complainant, the alleged harasser, and the organization. Breaches of confidentiality can expose organizations to legal liability for privacy-related torts. Leaks of information can also damage careers or reputations, as well as undermine confidence and trust in the employer. Preventing unnecessary disclosure can prevent individuals from being labeled complainers or harassers while the investigation is pending.

The assurance of confidentiality can be expressed in a variety of ways. The policy may state:

- Any allegation of harassment or retaliation that is brought to the attention of (name of investigator) will result in a mandatory, confidential investigation of the incident.
- All reports of harassment and subsequent investigations will be handled discreetly to avoid embarrassment for persons making the report and for subjects of their complaints.
- Any report of sex-based harassment will be treated discreetly and promptly investigated.

The policy should also acknowledge that the investigatory process will often necessitate some exceptions to the confidentiality rule, as in the following examples:

- All reports of sexual harassment shall be kept in confidence, except as is necessary to investigate the complaint and to respond to any related legal and/or administrative proceedings.
- [T]o the extent practical and appropriate under the circumstances, confidentiality will be maintained.

Organizational size and culture may affect the need for confidentiality protections. In a small business, the alleged harasser, the complainant, the person who receives the complaint, and the person who maintains records or files may constitute the entire business. As a practical matter, what makes sense in one workplace might require a different approach in another.

2. The Investigation Process

The need for flexibility to deal with unusual situations on a case-by-case basis should not preclude an organization from describing its general procedures for investigating a complaint and strictly adhering to those procedures. Failure to follow prescribed procedures can expose an organization to liability.

Many policies indicate that the investigation will involve all employees who may know of the alleged incident or similar problems and that the process will be thoroughly documented. The policy should also identify the investigators. For example:

> The complaint will be handled and resolved by the person to whom the complaint is reported, along with involvement and review by management.

Employers should be aware that written records of the investigation may be discoverable in any legal proceedings that might arise from the actions at issue. The following checklist suggests instructions that may be useful in conducting the investigation.

- Confirm the name and position of the person(s) alleged to be the victim of harassment, if the complaint is being raised by a third party.
- Identify the person(s) allegedly responsible for the harassment as well as any witnesses.
- Interview the complainant. Obtain as many details as possible. Ask open-ended, non-judgmental questions.
- Obtain information about the dates, frequency, and location of the alleged harassment.
- Ask complainants how they felt about the alleged harassment at the time it occurred.
- Ask complainants how they feel now and what resolution they would prefer, but advise them that their preferred resolution may not be the end result.
- Ask complainants for any supporting documents, e-mails, or other information.
- Inform complainants that a thorough and fair investigation will be conducted but that the employer may not be able to provide full details about the outcome of the investigation. Explain why not.
- Ask complainants whether they have told anyone else about the alleged harassment. If so, obtain the details concerning who, what, when, where, and the response, if any. Interview these individuals, as well as others whom complainants believe may have relevant information.

- Ask complainants whether anyone witnessed the alleged harassment.
- Determine whether alleged harassers have control over the compensation, working conditions, or future employment of complainants.
- Determine whether alleged harassers made or carried out any threats or promises in connection with the alleged harassment.
- Determine whether anyone knows of other victims of harassment by the same person. Interview these individuals.
- Determine what the organization's management knew, if anything, about the situation or other harassing conduct by the same individual.
- Interview the person(s) charged with harassment. Describe the charges and request a response. Invite a written statement as well as an oral explanation.
- Ask alleged harassers whether anyone else observed the conduct at issue or whether they discussed it with anyone else. Interview those individuals.
- Ask alleged harassers whether they have ever been subject to similar complaints. Check their personnel records.
- Provide a detailed report. Include all written documents.
- Recommend a response to the complaint, including sanctions for any conduct violating the organization's harassment policy. Consider complainant's preferences, alleged harasser's prior history, and the disposition of any similar previous cases.
- Submit the report to the designated decision maker. That individual should assess its adequacy and request any necessary additions or modifications. The decision maker should conduct any further interviews that would be helpful in resolving the matter and should document all actions.

PART V

RESOLVING THE COMPLAINT

When the investigation is complete, the decision maker should inform the complainant and advise him or her of the general outcome. If the investigation revealed inappropriate behavior and/or harassment, advise the complainant that the organization took appropriate, remedial action to avoid future incidents of this type of behavior. If the employer could not substantiate a finding of harassment, the decision-maker should advise the complainant of this as well. The amount of information provided may vary depending on the privacy concerns of those involved.

A. Sanctions

A policy on sex-based harassment should state the range of potential sanctions for such misconduct. It should also note that the organization will make every effort to deal with sex-based harassment by third parties, such as clients or vendors. The employer should develop procedures for dealing with such conduct. The severity of the sanctions should take into account whether the alleged harasser had any prior violations of the organization's harassment or discrimination policies, and whether there were any retaliatory responses or refusals to cooperate in connection with the current investigation. Appropriate corrective and disciplinary actions include:

- Review and retraining of the alleged harasser on all sex harassment and antiretaliation policies;
- Written reprimand;
- Referral to appropriate counseling;

- Withholding of a promotion;
- Demotion or reassignment;
- Financial penalties;
- Other non-monetary penalties;
- Temporary suspension; and
- Termination.

The employer should consider the severity of the harassing conduct and/or prior offenses when determining the appropriate severity of the discipline. The policy should clearly state that the organization will impose appropriate sanctions up to and including termination.

B. False Accusations

A well-drafted policy on sex-based harassment should recognize the damage that can result from false charges. Some organizations include provisions such as:

> False accusations of sexual harassment can have serious effects on innocent persons. If an investigation results in a finding that a person who has accused another of sexual harassment has maliciously, recklessly, or intentionally made false accusations, the accuser will be subject to appropriate sanctions, including discharge.

However, the employer should recognize that such policies may have the effect of deterring reports of questionable harassment. To encourage employees to come forward to report actions they believe to be sex-based harassment, some employers include provisions such as:

> Employees who make good faith reports of sex harassment are protected under this policy even if it turns out that the behavior at issue did not rise to the level of illegal sex harassment.

PART VI

MAINTAINING WRITTEN RECORDS OF COMPLAINTS

It is important for organizations to maintain a complete written record of each complaint and how the organization investigated and resolved the complaint. Documentation is key to proving that an employer conducted a prompt and thorough investigation in response to a complaint of harassment. This procedure will facilitate handling questions that may arise later in connection with a specific complaint or prior complaints against the same individual. It will also provide organizations with a record of how it handled different situations to ensure similar treatment of similar complaints. Employers should make sure that their procedures comply with any relevant state laws concerning personnel records. For example, some states require employers and/or public institutions to grant employees full access to their personnel files. Thus, to include full documentation of the entire investigation in the complainant's personnel file could expose the identity of witnesses and other confidential information. A well-drafted policy might include a provision on record-keeping such as:

> The organization will retain confidential documentation of all sex harassment allegations and investigations involving claims of sex harassment.

The policy should specify who will maintain the records. In some organizations, this responsibility may vary depending on the identity of the complainant and the alleged harasser. Some policies also specify the contents of the records and a double-blind filing system. Such a system identifies complainants in a file apart from the file on the documentation or resolution of the complaint in order to maintain their privacy. Some policies indicate the length of time that files will be kept before being destroyed (e.g., 10 years from the date of resolution, unless new circumstances dictate that they be kept longer). It is generally desirable to maintain files for at least a decade so that indications of any pattern of harassment or lack thereof are available.

PART VII

EDUCATION AND TRAINING

Effective implementation of a policy on sex-based harassment requires a comprehensive education and review process. Views differ about the cost-effectiveness of requiring specific sex-based harassment training programs for all employees, but employers should check state laws, as some states require regular training of employees.[1] At a minimum, however, educational materials and a copy of the policy should be included in all organizational handbooks, orientation publications, and related documents and should be distributed to all personnel. Training should also be mandatory for those directly involved in administering the harassment policy and those who have violated its terms. A wide range of resources are now available to assist in the development of an effective educational program. A representative sample is included in the bibliography in Appendix II.

The following steps will help to ensure effective implementation of a policy on sex-based harassment.

- Provide, at a minimum, a review of the sex harassment policy with all employees.

---

1. Laura Gatland, *Sexual Harassment: An Ounce of Prevention*, PERSPECTIVES, Fall 1998, at 6; Susan Bisom-Rapp, *Fixing Watches with Sledgehammers: The Questionable Embrace of Employees' Sexual Harassment Training by the Legal Profession*, 24 U. ARK. L. REV. 147 (2001); Susan Bisom-Rapp, *An Ounce of Prevention Is a Poor Substitute for a Pound of Cure: Confronting the Developing Jurisprudence of Education and Prevention in Employment Discrimination Law*, 22 BERKELEY J. EMP. & LAB. L. 11 (2001); Linda Hamilton Krieger & Susan T. Fiske, *Behavioral Realism in Employment Discrimination Law: Implicit Bias and Disparate Treatment*, 94 C.A.L.R. 997, 1018 (2006).

- Provide specific training for all individuals who are responsible for enforcing the policy. These more specific educational programs should include general information about the causes and consequences of sex-based harassment, what the individual should do once he or she receives a complaint, and how the organization will investigate any such complaints.
- Include a training session about sex-based harassment as part of the orientation for new lawyers and other new employees.
- Establish easy and inexpensive ways to detect sex-based harassment so that the organization is not simply relying on complaints. For example, ask about sex-based harassment in anonymous employee surveys and exit interviews.
- Mainstream the policy by making offensive conduct and sensitivity to diversity-related issues a factor in performance evaluation.
- Be proactive in dealing with individuals who have a reputation of engaging in harassment. The law requires employers to take prompt, remedial action to deal with any sex-based harassment of which they have, or should have had, knowledge. An organization should not wait for a formal complaint before responding to known misconduct. Inaction may be considered condonation and/or ratification and may also result in legal liability.
- Take steps to minimize any overreaction to the fear of harassment charges. As noted earlier, concerns about the appearance of impropriety or an unintentional offense have reportedly deterred some men from working closely with women colleagues and from including them in travel, client entertainment, and informal social events.

Policies and training on sex-based harassment should address issues of potential overreaction and the sex-based discrimination or retaliation that may result. Those responsible for work allocation and mentoring efforts should also be sensitive to the possibility of bias. Individuals should have equal opportunity and access to professional opportunities regardless of their gender.

PART VIII

CONCLUSION

A profession responsible for upholding the rule of law has a special obligation to ensure that its own conduct conforms to legal mandates. Moreover, as women enter the profession in equal numbers to men, no organization can afford conduct that denies equal opportunity on the basis of gender. Employers who want to ensure a productive workplace and to protect themselves from liability for sex harassment and/or gender discrimination suits need thorough and effective policies on sex-based harassment. Developing, implementing, and evaluating such policies should be a key priority in all legal workplaces.

APPENDIX I
SAMPLE POLICY: SEX-BASED HARASSMENT

Organizational Statement of Philosophy

This organization is committed to maintaining a professional work environment that is free of bias, prejudice, or harassment. Sex-based harassment is illegal. This organization will not tolerate sex-based harassment in the office, at work assignments outside the office, at office-sponsored social functions, or in any context subject to the organization's control.

Definition of Sex-Based Harassment

For purposes of this policy, sex-based harassment is defined as unwelcome verbal or physical conduct of a sexual or gender-based nature when: 1) submission to or rejection of this conduct is used as a factor in decisions affecting hiring, evaluation, promotion, or other aspects of employment; 2) this conduct substantially interferes with an individual's employment or creates an intimidating, hostile, or offensive work environment. Examples of sex-based harassment include, but are not limited to:

- Demands for sexual favors in exchange for continued employment or favorable reviews, assignments, commendations, or promotions;
- Continued or repeated sexual jokes, epithets, advances, or propositions;
- Verbal abuse of a sexual nature or of a hostile nature directed at one sex;
- Graphic verbal commentary about sexual prowess, attractiveness, or deficiencies;
- Sexually degrading or vulgar descriptions of another individual;
- Leering, whistling, touching, pinching, or assaults;
- Suggestive, insulting, or obscene comments or gestures;

- Coercive sexual acts;
- Workplace displays of sexually suggestive objects, computer screens, pictures, posters, graffiti, or cartoons;
- Questions about sexual conduct, sexual orientation, or sexual preferences;
- Hostile, demeaning, or intimidating conduct that is consistently targeted at only one sex, even if the content is not sexual;
- Electronic transmission or display of sexually explicit, demeaning, or hostile materials;
- Unwillingness to train, assist, or cooperate with another colleague on the basis of sex;
- Destruction or sabotage of work on the basis of sex; and
- Retaliation against employees for complaining about such behaviors.

This behavior is unacceptable in the workplace and in other work-related settings such as business trips, court appearances, law school hiring functions, and business-related social events.

Individuals Covered Under the Policy

This policy covers all employees (associates, staff attorneys, paralegals, support staff, any other employee of the organization) and partners. The organization will not tolerate sex-based harassment by any member, employee, or third person including clients, opposing counsel, court personnel, or vendors who conduct business with this organization. The organization requires reporting of all incidents of sex-based harassment, regardless of who the offender may be.

Reporting a Complaint

The organization requires individuals who believe they are being sexually harassed to notify the offender clearly and promptly that this behavior is unwelcome. However, the organization also recognizes that disparities of power and status or perceptions of those disparities may make such a confrontation difficult. When the individual does not feel comfortable notifying the harasser that his or her behavior is unwelcome or when the problems are not resolved through informal, direct communication, the individual should make a formal complaint under the procedures set forth below. Simply discussing the problem with a co-worker is neither effective nor sufficient.

1. Notification of Alleged Harassment

Individuals who believe they have been subjected to sex-based harassment should report the incident to any member of the committee listed below. [Add committee members].[1] Such report may be verbal or written, but if written, should be delivered in such a way as to preserve confidentiality.

An individual also may report the complaint to his/her supervisor or any other member of management. If the supervisor or manager successfully resolves the complaint in an informal manner, he or she must file a confidential report to [organization management or designated individual] about the complaint and resolution so that the organization will be aware of any pattern of harassment by a particular individual. A supervisor or manager who has not had special training in dealing with sex-based harassment complaints must be required to consult a member of the organization's committee or a member of human resources before taking action.

2. Description of Misconduct

An accurate record of objectionable behavior or misconduct is necessary to resolve a formal complaint of sex-based harassment. Verbal reports of sex-based harassment must be reduced to writing by either the complainant or the individual who receives the complaint and should be signed by the complainant. Individuals who believe they have been harassed should maintain a record of objectionable conduct in order to corroborate their allegations. Likewise, any supervisor or manager who receives a report of sex harassment should thoroughly document the report, being sure to include a detailed description of the alleged conduct and any witnesses thereto.

While the organization encourages individuals to keep written notes in order to record offensive conduct accurately, they should be aware that if a lawsuit develops from the reported incident, their notes may not be considered privileged information and, therefore, may not be kept confidential in the event of litigation.

3. Time Frame for Reporting Complaint

The organization requires a prompt reporting of complaints so that a timely response and appropriate action may be taken. Therefore,

---

1. In smaller organizations, a committee may not be feasible. In that situation, simply delete the references to the committee.

once a supervisor or manager receives a complaint of sex harassment, he or she should contact the committee, managing partner, in-house counsel, or human resources. However, due to the sensitivity of these problems, late reporting of complaints will not prevent appropriate remedial action.

4. **Protection Against Retaliation**
The organization will not in any way retaliate against an individual who makes a report of sex-based harassment nor permit any partner or employee to do so. Retaliation is a serious violation of this sex-based harassment policy and should be reported immediately. Any person found to have retaliated against another individual for reporting sex-based harassment and/or for participating in an investigation of sex harassment will be subject to the same disciplinary action provided for other forms of harassment described below, up to and including termination.

Investigating the Complaint

1. **Confidentiality**
Any allegation of sex-based harassment brought to the attention of [the organization's appointed committee] will be promptly investigated in a confidential manner so as to protect the privacy of persons involved. The organization will maintain confidentiality throughout the investigatory process to the extent practical and appropriate under the circumstances.

2. **Identification of Investigators**
The organization will determine the person best suited to conduct the investigation [committee, human resources personnel, managing partner, in-house counsel, other management-level personnel and/or a neutral member of the organization's administration]. In addition, any of the following individuals may be included in reviewing the investigation and outcome: [list appropriate individuals].

3. **Investigation Procedures**
[Do not include this section in the policy that is distributed to all employees—it is really a guide for the investigators.]
In conducting investigations, organization personnel will consider the wishes of the complainant but should thoroughly investigate the matter as they believe necessary. The complainant should

be informed as to the status of the investigation. Steps to be taken in the investigation include:

- Confirm the name and position of persons complaining.
- Identify the person(s) responsible for the alleged harassment as well as any witnesses.
- Interview complainants. Attempt to get as many details as possible. Ask open-ended, non-judgmental questions.
- Obtain information about the dates, frequency, and location of the alleged harassment.
- Ask complainants how they felt about the alleged harassment at the time it occurred.
- Ask complainants how they feel now and what resolution they would prefer, but advise them that their preferred resolution may not be the result.
- Inform complainants that a thorough and fair investigation will be conducted but that the employer may not be able to provide full details about the outcome of the investigation, and explain why not.
- Ask complainants whether they have told anyone else about the incidents of harassment. If so, obtain the details concerning who, what, when, where, and the response, if any. Interview these individuals, as well as others who complainants believe may have relevant information.
- Determine whether alleged harassers have control over the compensation, working conditions, or future employment of complainants.
- Determine whether alleged harassers made or carried out any threats or promises in connection with the alleged harassment.
- Assure the complainant that the alleged harasser is prohibited from retaliating against him or her, and direct the complainant to report any retaliation to the person(s) conducting the investigation immediately.
- Determine whether anyone knows of other victims of harassment by the same person. Interview these individuals.
- Determine what the organization's management knew, if anything, about the situation or other harassing conduct by the same individual.
- Interview persons charged with harassment. Describe the charges and request a response. Invite a written statement as well as an oral explanation.

- Ask alleged harassers whether anyone else observed the conduct at issue or whether they discussed it with anyone else. Interview those individuals.
- Ask alleged harassers whether they have ever been subject to similar complaints. Check their personnel records.
- Provide a detailed report. Include all written documents.
- Recommend responses to complaints, including sanctions for any conduct violating the organization's harassment policy. Consider complainants' preferences, alleged harassers' prior history, and the disposition of any similar, previous cases.
- Submit the report to the designated decision-maker. That individual should assess its adequacy and request any necessary additions or modifications. The decision maker should conduct any interviews that would be helpful in resolving the matter and document all actions.

Resolving the Complaint

Upon completing the investigation of a sex-based harassment complaint, the organization will communicate its findings and intended actions to the complainant and the alleged harasser. If the review committee finds that a violation of this policy has occurred, the offender will be subject to appropriate disciplinary procedures, as listed below. If the review committee determines that no violation has occurred, this finding will be communicated to the complainant in an appropriately sensitive manner. In certain circumstances, the organization may require the alleged harasser to review the sex harassment policy and/or attend additional sex harassment training.

1. Sanctions

Individuals found to have violated this policy will be sanctioned, up to and including discharge. Appropriate sanctions will be determined by [select the appropriate individual or group of individuals]. At a minimum, any violation will result in a formal reprimand and written record. Additional action may include: review and retraining the alleged harasser on all sex harassment and antiretaliation policies; referral to appropriate counseling; withholding of a promotion; demotion or reassignment; financial penalties; other non-monetary penalties; temporary suspension; and/or termination.

Although the organization has limited ability to control sex-based harassment by third parties such as clients, opposing counsel, or vendors, any individual who has experienced sex-based harassment should file a complaint and be assured that action will be taken.

2. **False Accusations**

If an investigation results in a finding that the complainant falsely accused another of sex-based harassment intentionally or maliciously, the complainant will be subject to appropriate sanctions, including any of those specified for harassment. However, employees who make good faith reports of sex harassment are protected under this policy even if it turns out that the behavior at issue did not rise to the level of illegal sex harassment.

Maintaining a Written Record of the Complaint

The organization shall complete a written record of each complaint and how it was investigated and resolved. Written records shall be maintained in a confidential manner in the office of [name the appropriate individual or appropriate division within the office].

Written records shall be retained for 10 years from the date of the resolution unless new circumstances dictate that the file should be kept for a longer period of time. A double-blind filing system will be used, with the names of the complainants in a separate record from the resolution of the complaint in order to maximize protection of their privacy.

Conclusion

[Organization name] has developed this policy to ensure that all its members and employees can work in an environment free from sex-based harassment. The organization will make every effort to ensure that all its personnel are familiar with the policy and that complaints are promptly and thoroughly investigated and appropriately resolved.

APPENDIX II SELECTED BIBLIOGRAPHY ON SEX-BASED HARASSMENT

Books, Manuals, Kits, Tapes, and Videos

ALI-ABA, *Sexual Harassment Update*, Audiotapes, 1998.

Francis Achampong, *Workplace Sexual Harassment Law: Principles, Landmark Developments, and Framework for Effective Risk Management*, Westport, Conn.: Quorum, 1999.

Maria Arapakis, *Sexual Harassment—How to Protect Yourself and Your Organization*, Videotapes, Boulder, Colo.: Career Track Publications, 1993.

Bureau of National Affairs (BNA), *Preventing Sexual Harassment: A Fact Sheet for Employees*, Washington, D.C.: BNA, 2001.

Benokraitis, Nijole V., *Subtle Sexism*, Thousand Oaks, Cal.: Sage Publications, 1997.

Margaret A. Crouch, *Thinking About Sexual Harassment: A Guide for the Perplexed*, New York: Oxford University Press, 2001.

Raymond F. Gregory, *Unwelcome and Unlawful: Sexual Harassment in the American Workplace*, Ithaca, N.Y.: Cornell University Press, 2004.

Maureen Harrison & Steve Gilbert, *Sexual Harassment Decisions of the United States Supreme Court*, Carlsbad, Cal.: Excellent Books, 2006.

Linda LeMoncheck & James P. Sterba, eds., *Sexual Harassment: Issues and Answers*, New York, N.Y.: Oxford University Press, 2001.

Anne Levy, *Workplace Sexual Harassment*, Upper Saddle River, N.J.: Prentice Hall, 2d ed., 2002.

Marshall, Anna-Maria, *Confronting Sexual Harassment: The Law and Politics of Everyday Life*, Burlington, Vt.: Ashgate Publishing Co., 2005.

Darlene Orlov & Michael T. Roumell, *What Every Manager Needs to Know About Sexual Harassment*, New York, N.Y.: American Management Association, 2005.

Tracy O'Shea & Jane LaLonde, *Sexual Harassment: A Practical Guide to the Law, Your Rights, and Your Options for Taking Action*, New York: St. Martin's Griffin, 1998.

M.A. Paludi & R.B. Barickman, *Sexual Harassment, Work, and Education: A Resource Manual for Prevention*, Albany, N.Y.: State University of New York Press, 1998.

Michele Paludi & Carmen Paludi, *Academic and Workplace Sexual Harassment: A Handbook of Cultural, Social Science, Management, and Legal Perspectives*, Westport, Conn.: Praeger Publishers, 2003.

William Petrocelli & Barbara Kate Repa, *Sexual Harassment: An Employers Prevention Guide*, Berkeley, Cal.: Nolo Press, 1999.

William Petrocelli & Barbara Kate Repa, *Sexual Harassment on the Job*, Berkeley, Cal.: Nolo Press, 4th ed. 1999.

Patricia Reuss & Bob Applegate, et al., eds., *Renaissance 5809: Preventing Sexual Harassment*, Renaissance Professional Training, 2005.

Deborah L. Rhode, *Speaking of Sex: The Denial of Gender Inequality*, Cambridge, Mass.: Harvard University Press, 1997.

Matthew B. Schiff & Linda C. Kramer, eds., *Litigating the Sexual Harassment Case*, Chicago, IL: American Bar Association, 2000.

The Human Equation, Inc., *Preventing and Managing Sexual Harassment*, The Human Equation, Inc., 2000.

Susan Webb, *Step Forward: Sexual Harassment in the Workplace*, New York: Mastermedia, 2nd ed. 1998.

Susan Webb, *Sexual Harassment . . . Shades of Gray*, Video Training Package, Five videotapes, the Resource Manual, the Training Manual, a Leader's Guide, and 25 participant handbooks. Seattle, Wash.: Pacific Resource Development Group, 1999.

Paul Weizer, *Sexual Harassment: Cases, Case Studies, and Commentary*, New York: Peter Lang Publishing Group, 2002.

Paul I. Weizer, *The Supreme Court and Sexual Harassment: Preventing Harassment While Preserving Free Speech*, Lanham, Md.: Lexington Books, 2000.

Zero Tolerance: An Employer's Guide to Preventing Sexual Harassment & Healing the Workplace, Rockville, MD: BNA Communications, Inc., 1997.

Reports, Guidelines, Bibliographies, and Surveys

ABA Commission on Women in the Profession, *The Unfinished Agenda: A Report on the Status of Women in the Legal Profession*, 2001.

EEOC, *Facts About Sexual Harassment*, 1997.

EEOC, *Guidance on Vicarious Liability for Unlawful Harassment by Supervisors*, Daily Lab. Rep. *(BNA)* No. 118, June 18, 1999.

International Labour Office, *Annotated Bibliography on Sexual Harassment*, 1999.

Debra S. Katz & Alan R. Kabat, *Advanced Employment Law and Litigation: Sexual Harassment in the Workplace*, Washington, D.C.: ALI-ABA, 2002.

Martha S. West, *Preventing Sexual Harassment: The Federal Courts Wake-Up Call for Women*, 68 BROOKLYN L. REV. 457 (2002).

Web Sites

American Bar Association: http://www.abanet.org

ABA Commission on Women in the Profession: http://www.abanet.org/women

Employer-Employee: http://www.employer-employee.com/sexhar1.htm

Equal Employment Opportunity Commission, Facts About Sexual Harassment: http://www.eeoc.gov/facts/fs-sex.html

Feminist Majority Foundation, Sexual Harassment Internet Resources: http://www.feminist.org/911/harass.html

Legal Momentum (formerly NOW Legal Defense and Education Fund): http://www.legalmomentum.org

National Partnership for Women and Families: http://www.nationalpartnership.org

National Women's Law Center: http://www.nwlc.org

NOW and Sexual Harassment: http://www.now.org/issues/harass

Sexual Harassment Prevention Training Materials and Services: http://www.shadesofgray.com

Sexuality Information and Education Council of the United States: http://www.siecus.org